MAGELLAN AND DA GAMA
To the Far East and beyond

Clint Twist

Evans Brothers Limited

Evans Brothers Limited
2A Portman Mansions
Chiltern Street
London W1M 1LE

©Evans Brothers Limited 1993

All rights reserved. No part of this publication may be reproduced, stored in a retrieval system or transmitted in any form or by any means, electronic, mechanical, photocopying, recording or otherwise, without prior permission of Evans Brothers Limited.

Printed in Hong Kong

ISBN 0 237 51268 8

Series editor: Su Swallow
Editor: Nicola Barber
Designer: Neil Sayer
Production: Peter Thompson

Maps and Illustrations: Brian Watson, Linden Artists

Acknowledgements

For permission to reproduce copyright material the author and publishers gratefully acknowledge the following:

Cover (top left) Indonesian 'spirit banner', (middle) Benin head, (bottom left) Mogul mosque in Delhi, India, Robert Harding Picture Library, (bottom right) early mariner's compass, Michael Holford
Title page Juliet Highet, Hutchison Library
page 4 (left) Michael Holford, (right) Anthony Blake Photo Library **page 5** Ancient Art and Architecture Collection **page 6** Robert Harding Picture Library **page 8** (top) Academia das Ciencias de Lisboa, Robert Harding Picture Library, (bottom) Michael Holford **page 9** Robert Harding Picture Library **page 10** Robert Harding Picture Library **page 11** Robert Harding Picture Library **page 12** (top) Mary Evans Picture Library, (bottom) Crown copyright, Science Museum, Robert Harding Picture Library **page 13** National Maritime Museum, Robert Harding Picture Library **page 14** Robert Harding Picture Library **page 15** Nicola Wells, Life File **page 16** (top) David Heath, Life File, (bottom) John Fison, Life File **page 17** Eric Wilkins, Life File **page 18** Ronald Sheridan, Ancient Art and Architecture Collection **page 19** Robert Harding Picture Library **page 20** Werner Forman Archive **page 21** (top) Andrew Ward, Life File, (bottom) The Image Bank **page 22** Robert Harding Associates **page 23** (top) Timothy Beddow, Hutchison Library, (bottom) Michael Holford **page 24** (top) Crispin Hughes, Hutchison Library, (bottom) British Museum, Werner Forman Archive **page 25** (top) Robert Aberman, Barbara Heller, (bottom) Mo Khan, Life File **page 26** (top) Steve Jansen, Life File, (bottom) Ancient Art and Architecture Collection **page 27** Andrew Watson, Life File **page 28** Michael Holford **page 29** Mary Evans Picture Library **page 30** (top) Michael Holford, (bottom) Robert Harding Picture Library **page 31** (top) Robert Harding Picture Library, (bottom) J.G. Fuller, Hutchison Library, (inset) Michael Holford **page 32** Robert Harding Picture Library **page 33** (top) Tony Souter, Hutchison Library, (bottom) Private Collection, New York, USA, Werner Forman Archive, **page 34** K. Rodgers, Hutchison Library **page 35** (top) Jany Sauvanet, NHPA, (middle) Robert Harding Picture Library **page 36** Robert Harding Picture Library **page 37** Robert Harding Picture Library **page 38** (top) Sarah Murray, Hutchison Library, (bottom) Mary Evans Picture Library **page 39** Michael Holford **page 40** (main and inset) Robert Francis, Robert Harding Picture Library **page 41** National Maritime Museum **page 42** (top) Ronald Sheridan, Ancient Art and Architecture Collection, (bottom) Hutchison Library **page 43** Mary Evans Picture Library.

Contents

Introduction 4
The Age of Discovery ❖ Sailing to the East ❖ Expedition leaders

The historical background 6
A shift of power ❖ Islamic invaders ❖ Africa revealed
Tropical treasure ❖ Henry the Navigator ❖ Spanish America
Portuguese India ❖ Rivals for world power ❖ The spice trade

Ships and sailors 12
A choice of ships ❖ The carrack ❖ Da Gama's fleet
Leading an expedition ❖ Medical problems ❖ Magellan's fleet
Equipping for voyage ❖ Native craft ❖ The age of the carrack

The voyages of Vasco da Gama 18
A royal send off ❖ An unusual route ❖ East Africa
To India ❖ Homeward bound ❖ Success and disaster

Local cultures - Africa and India 22
Africa ❖ The Portuguese ❖ West African states
Forest kingdoms ❖ East Africa ❖ India ❖ Cities and religions
Invasions and empires ❖ Hinduism ❖ The arrival of Islam

The voyage of Ferdinand Magellan 28
'Rights of rope and knife' ❖ Daggers at midnight
The Strait of Magellan ❖ Pacific islands ❖ The battle on the beach
A perilous return

Local cultures - Patagonia and the Pacific 34
The land of big feet ❖ Filipino culture ❖ The people of the Pacific
The Spice Islands

What happened later 38
The Portuguese empire ❖ Mercantile capitalism ❖ Spanish concerns
The Dutch revolt ❖ Spain defeated ❖ Empires in India
An English merchant-adventurer ❖ The Catholic empires

Glossary 44

Index 44

Introduction

The Age of Discovery

The 16th century is often called the Age of Discovery. During this period, European seafarers set out across unknown waters and sailed around the world for the first time. As a result, Europe was transformed from a wealthy but inward-looking region into the powerful centre of worldwide empires. The conquest of the oceans during the 16th century enabled European commerce and culture to spread rapidly to all parts of the planet.

Sailing to the East

The Age of Discovery actually began during the late 15th century with the first voyage of Christopher Columbus in 1492. Before Columbus sailed, Europeans had no idea that America existed. In fact, Columbus was searching for a sea route to the East when he arrived in America by mistake. The accidental discovery of America brought unexpected riches to the rulers of Spain, who paid for Columbus's voyage. But it brought Europe no closer to the East – the wealthy countries of Japan, China and India described by Marco Polo 200 years earlier. The search for a sea route to the East continued, and within only 30 years of

An African view of Europeans, this salt cellar was carved in Nigeria towards the end of the 15th century. Above the figures is a replica of a Portuguese ship, complete with a lookout in the crow's nest.

Marco Polo described the East as the source of spices such as nutmeg (top left), pepper and cloves (2nd row left and right), and cinnamon (bottom left).

Ferdinand Magellan and Vasco da Gama

The Belém Tower in Lisbon stands near the place from which da Gama set sail in 1497. Standing out in the River Tagus, it was the landmark that homecoming sailors longed to see.

Columbus's first voyage, two other Europeans achieved what Columbus had failed to do.

In 1497, Vasco da Gama sailed around the tip of Africa and to India and back, establishing a Portuguese empire in the East. Twenty-five years later, a ship from the fleet of Ferdinand Magellan finally returned to Spain, having sailed right around the world. Spain was established as the leading naval power in Europe, with Portugal a close second.

Expedition leaders

Vasco da Gama was a professional Portuguese navigator, trained by the best experts in Europe. Because of his skills and training, he was chosen to lead the final stage of Portugal's 70-year exploration of the African coast and the Indian Ocean. Later in his career, he was appointed to rule India on behalf of the Portuguese king.

Ferdinand Magellan was also Portuguese by birth. As a young man he had a successful career as a soldier, but he later quarrelled with the king and left Portugal. Magellan then went to work in Spain, which was Portugal's only serious rival at this time. On behalf of Spain, Magellan set out on the most ambitious voyage of the Age of Discovery. His aim was to sail around the world. Some of his crew were successful, but Magellan was killed midway through the voyage.

Horizons

After reading this book, you may want to find out more about some aspect of da Gama's and Magellan's discoveries. Or you may become interested in a particular place or topic. At the end of some of the chapters you will find **Horizons** boxes. These list the names of people that are not mentioned in this book, but which are nevertheless part of the story of Vasco da Gama and Ferdinand Magellan. By looking them up in the indexes of other reference books, you will be able to discover more about da Gama's and Magellan's world.

The historical background

A shift of power

Since the days of the Roman Empire the Mediterranean Sea had been the centre of European attention. The Mediterranean was Europe's only access to the silks, spices and other luxury goods that came from the East. Most of this cargo arrived at Venice which became extremely rich as a result of trade with the East. The countries of the Atlantic coast, far from the centre of this wealthy trade, remained on the fringes of European affairs.

During the Age of Discovery, this situation changed. In fact all the countries that ruled the seas during the 16th century also had easy access to the Atlantic Ocean – Portugal and Spain, and later France, England and the Netherlands. Long experience of the ocean winds and weather gave sailors from these countries an advantage over those who learned their sailing in the Mediterranean Sea. As a result, the Atlantic countries found themselves at the centre of a new transoceanic world.

Islamic invaders

Both Spain and Portugal had been conquered at the beginning of the 7th century by the Moors, Islamic invaders from North Africa. The Christian reconquest began about 200 years later, but progress was slow. Spain was not completely free from Islamic rule until 1492, the same year that Columbus set sail. By this time, Spain had a powerful navy operating from ports throughout the Mediterranean.

The Atlantic coast is Portugal's only coastline,

The interior of the cathedral at Cordoba, in Spain. The building was originally an Islamic mosque, but it was converted to a cathedral after the Islamic Moors had been driven out of southern Spain.

Portuguese fishermen mend their nets by hand on the beach. They fish the stormy waters of the Atlantic exactly as fishermen did in da Gama's day.

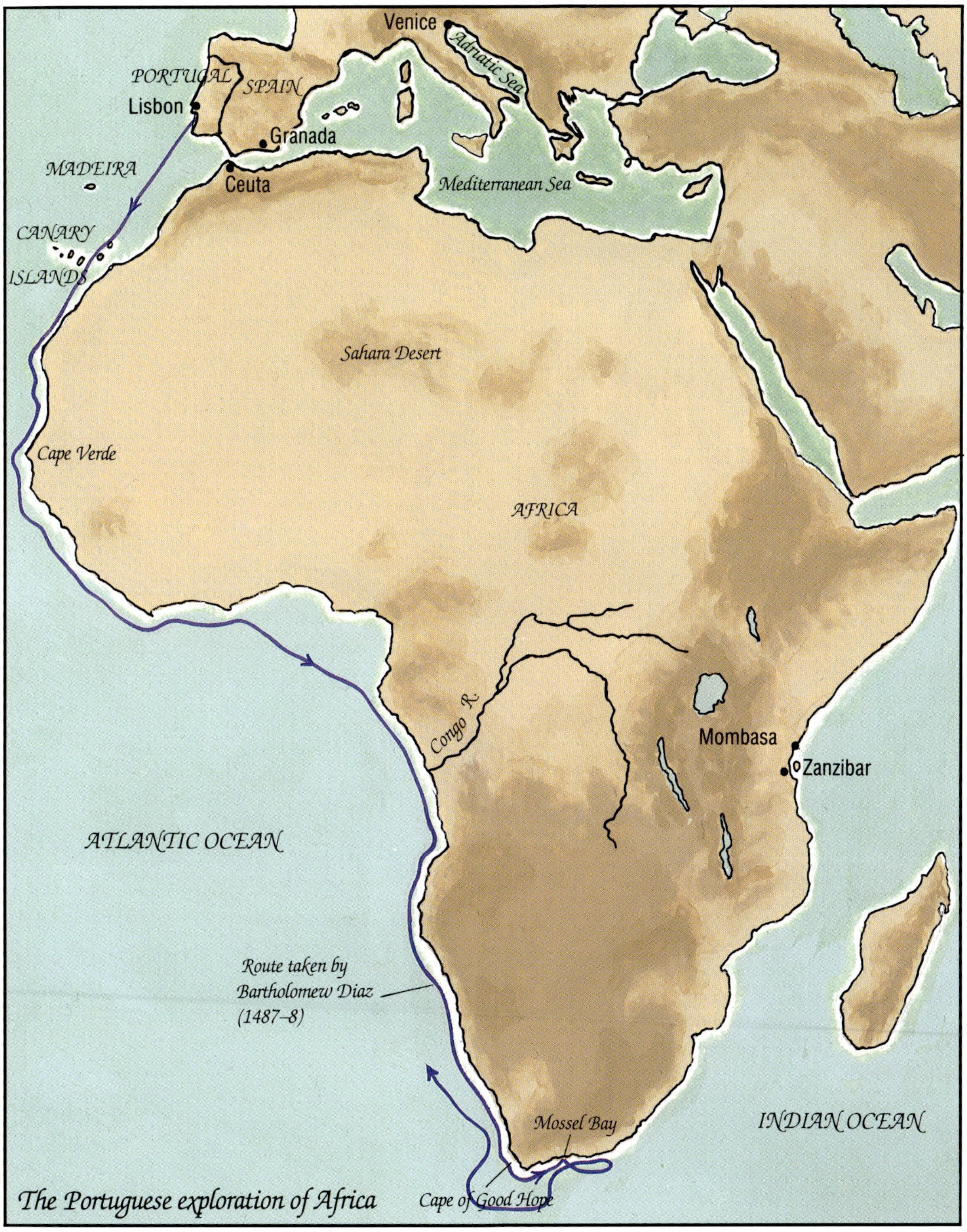

The Portuguese exploration of Africa

Route taken by Bartholomew Diaz (1487–8)

so Portuguese sailors had no alternative but to venture out into the ocean. Fishing and coastal trade became an important part of the Portuguese economy. It is not surprising that Portuguese kings paid particular attention to exploring the Atlantic Ocean. What is surprising is the amount that the Portuguese were willing to learn from their Islamic enemies. By studying Islamic methods, the Portuguese quickly became the best navigators in Europe.

Africa revealed

In 1139, Portugal was at last declared a Christian kingdom once more, although the southern province of the Algarve was not recaptured until 1250. Once Portugal was finally free from Islamic rule, and while parts of Spain were still occupied by the Moors,

A 16th-century map illustrating Portugal's discoveries in Africa up to 1475. While this map shows a detailed knowledge of the coastline, the interior of Africa remained completely unknown to Europeans for many years.

the Portuguese turned their attention to overseas exploration. Their first great success came in 1415, when they captured Ceuta, a Moroccan port close to the Straits of Gibraltar. Having established a base at Ceuta, the Portuguese proceeded to sail farther along the African coast. In 1419, Portuguese ships reached the island of Madeira, and in 1431, the Azores, farther west. These waters were well known to Islamic sailors, and the Portuguese eagerly examined the charts that they captured from them. Soon, however, the Portuguese explorers ventured into uncharted waters. In 1445, Portuguese ships sailed around Cape Verde, the western tip of Africa; and by 1460, they had reached the land that is present-day Sierra Leone.

Some time during the next 20 years, European ships first sailed south of the equator, and by 1482 there was a Portuguese fleet anchored at the mouth of the Congo River. The Portuguese made good use of the skills they had learned from Islamic navigators, and produced accurate charts of the African coast. But geographical knowledge was only one of the trophies that Portuguese ships took home. Africa was also found to be rich in other ways, in particular as a source of gold, and of slaves.

Tropical treasure

Tropical Africa, south of the Sahara desert, made a tremendous impression on the first European explorers because it was so different from anything they had experienced before. Black people themselves were not a novelty – black people had lived in European cities since the days of the Roman Empire. However, African culture was a complete shock to the Europeans. Throughout their history the Portuguese, their European

Henry the Navigator

Prince Henry of Portugal (1394-1460) was born in the last years of the 14th century, yet his influence was to extend to the 16th century and beyond. As the youngest son of the Portuguese king, Henry was not expected to inherit the throne, so he was free to follow his own interests which included exploring. Until his death, Prince Henry was the guiding force behind the Portuguese exploration of Africa. He organised most of the voyages, although he himself remained at home in Portugal.

Henry turned European navigation into an exact science. He set up a school for sea captains and navigators where students were taught by the best astronomers and mathematicians in Europe. Henry was also a keen collector of maps and charts, especially Islamic charts that showed waters unfamiliar to the Christians. Under his direction, Portuguese navigators drew accurate maps of the newly-explored African coastline. As a result of his involvement with the sea, this land-bound prince earned a nickname: Henry the Navigator.

Prince Henry, pictured here as a scholar

neighbours, and their Islamic foes, had all shared a common cultural background. For the first time in thousands of years, Europeans now encountered people from an entirely different type of culture.

Disappointingly, despite its novelty, Africa contained none of the spices, silks, rubies or emeralds described by Marco Polo. However, in West Africa the Portuguese made the same discovery that the merchants and traders from Arabia had long since made in East Africa – that Africa seemed to have an endless supply of gold. The native peoples were happy to trade their gold for brightly coloured cloth, cheap iron knives, glass beads and other manufactured goods. In fact, most of this gold had been gathered over many centuries, and the supply soon began to run out. But when gold was difficult to find, native African rulers were happy to trade captured prisoners instead. The first cargo of black slaves was taken back to Portugal in 1441.

In 1479 the Portuguese persuaded the Pope to grant them exclusive rights to the seas south of the Canary Islands. This meant that other nations were banned from sailing down the African coast. In 1487-8, the Portuguese captain, Bartholomew Diaz, sailed around the southern tip of Africa, and into the Indian Ocean. A sea route to India had at last been discovered, and only Portuguese ships could use it.

Spanish America

This was the situation that faced Spain at the beginning of the 1490s. The Spanish were being prevented from taking part in the newly developing worldwide trade by their rivals, the Portuguese. In other ways, Spain was experiencing a revival at this time. Most

Tenerife in the Canary Islands. These islands have been controlled by Spain since the 15th century.

of the land under Islamic rule had been recaptured, and only the Moorish fortress of Granada still held out against the Christian armies. Spanish pride demanded a success overseas. The Spanish king and queen were at last persuaded to agree to Christopher Columbus's scheme to sail westwards to find a route to the lands of the East.

When he sailed in 1492, Columbus found a land unknown to Europeans: America. This strange country, called the 'New World' by the Europeans, soon provided Spain with gold and silver in abundance.

Portuguese India

The Portuguese were shocked by Columbus's discovery. Anxiously, the Portuguese court awaited news of silks and spices arriving in Spain. Only gradually did the truth emerge – whatever it was that Columbus had discovered, it was not Japan, China or India. The great prize of a sea route to the East was still there for the Portuguese to take. In 1497 Vasco da Gama set sail for India, and he reached Calicut on the Indian coast in May 1498.

Following da Gama's success, the Portuguese established a long-distance trading empire that stretched halfway around the world. From China, India and Africa, Portuguese ships brought the treasures of the East back to Europe. The Portuguese did not try to conquer and rule their overseas territories. They were content to build fortified trading posts along the African and Indian coasts. From Zanzibar on the East African coast, to Hormuz at the entrance to the Persian Gulf and Calicut in India, Portuguese fortresses ringed the Indian Ocean; and the Portuguese navy patrolled the shipping routes to make sure that no rival ships threatened their trading rights.

Fort Jesus in Mombasa was constructed by the Portuguese between 1593-5.

Rivals for world power

At the beginning of the 16th century, Spain and Portugal were engaged in a bitter rivalry over sea power and foreign trade. Spain had discovered

The spice trade

During the time of the Roman Empire, Europe was introduced to pepper and other exotic spices from the East. These spices became very popular among those people that could afford them. By the end of the 15th century, Europe had developed a craze for spices. Pepper was the most popular, closely followed by cloves, ginger, nutmeg and cinnamon. Traditionally, Europe had obtained its spices from the merchants of Venice, who, in turn, traded with merchants in the Middle East where the overland spice routes from India ended. However, after Columbus's voyage the Spanish began to bring back chillies, capsicums and cayenne pepper from America. The Portuguese, too, entered the spice trade when they established direct contact with India and the Spice Islands (the present-day islands of the Moluccas in Indonesia). As a result, Venice's share in the spice trade declined rapidly.

Pepper growing in Sarawak, Malaysia. The unripe fruits are dried to form peppercorns.

America, but the Portuguese had found a sea route to India, and they controlled the spice trade.

The Spanish had other reasons to feel discontented. As the country that had paid for Columbus's voyages, Spain had naturally claimed all the newly discovered land to the west. In 1494, Spain insisted on making a treaty with Portugal in which Spain was granted the right to claim any lands west of a certain point in the mid-Atlantic. Unfortunately for Spain, this meant that Brazil (when it was discovered around 1500) was granted to Portugal. And despite having discovered a New World, Spanish ships were still only allowed to sail in the North Atlantic (see page 9). Only Portuguese ships were permitted to sail upon other, more distant oceans.

Once again, as in the case of Columbus, it was a discontented foreigner who provided the answer to Spain's problems. In 1519 a Portuguese captain, Ferdinand Magellan, set out with a Spanish fleet. His aim was to sail around the globe, to take over part of the spice trade, and to demonstrate to the whole world the supremacy of Spanish sea power.

Horizons

You could find out about these Europeans who all lived at about the same time as da Gama and Magellan: Charles V (king of Spain and Holy Roman Emperor); John Hawkins (an English sea captain); Afonso de Albuquerque (the Portuguese viceroy of India); Nicolas Copernicus (a Polish astronomer); Hernan Cortéz and Francisco Pizarro (Spanish conquistadors); the Medici family (Italian bankers).

Ships and sailors

Shipbuilding at the end of the 15th century

A choice of ships

The voyages of the Age of Discovery covered much greater distances than humans had ever travelled before. On da Gama's first voyage to India and back, he sailed more than 38,000 kilometres. The surviving ship of Magellan's fleet sailed a total of more than 45,000 kilometres to complete the first circumnavigation of the globe. Yet none of the ships used on these voyages was very big. The largest carried no more than 150 tonnes of cargo, and had about 60 crew. Many of the earlier discoveries were made in even smaller ships.

The Portuguese had used caravels to explore the African coastline. These were small craft averaging about 50 tonnes and with a crew of between 15 and 20 sailors. A typical caravel had two masts, fitted with triangular lateen sails which made the ship easy to manoeuvre when following an unknown coastline. The caravel's shallow draught made it ideal for navigating in coastal waters, yet caravels could also stand up to the rough waves in mid-ocean. Columbus made most of his discoveries in a caravel, the *Niña*.

However, the caravel did have disadvantages. While the lateen sails were ideal for changeable coastal winds, they were not so well suited to the steady winds found in mid-ocean. Square sails were more efficient, and were easier for the crew to handle. Caravels were also uncomfortably small, limiting the amount of food and fresh water that could be carried. Many expedition leaders preferred larger ships that could carry a bigger crew and more supplies. Larger ships also made better gun-platforms. To overcome the caravel's disadvantages, the Portuguese and Spanish navigators of the early 16th century chose instead to sail in a ship known as the carrack.

A model of a Portuguese caravel from about 1535

The carrack

The carrack was a development of the traditional Mediterranean merchant ship, with a wide hull designed to hold as much cargo as possible. The name carrack comes from an Arabic word *qaraqir* meaning 'merchant ships'. By the end of the 15th century, most carracks had at least three masts. The foremast and mainmast were rigged with square sails that made the best use of strong, steady winds. The smaller masts towards the stern of the ship had either square or lateen sails.

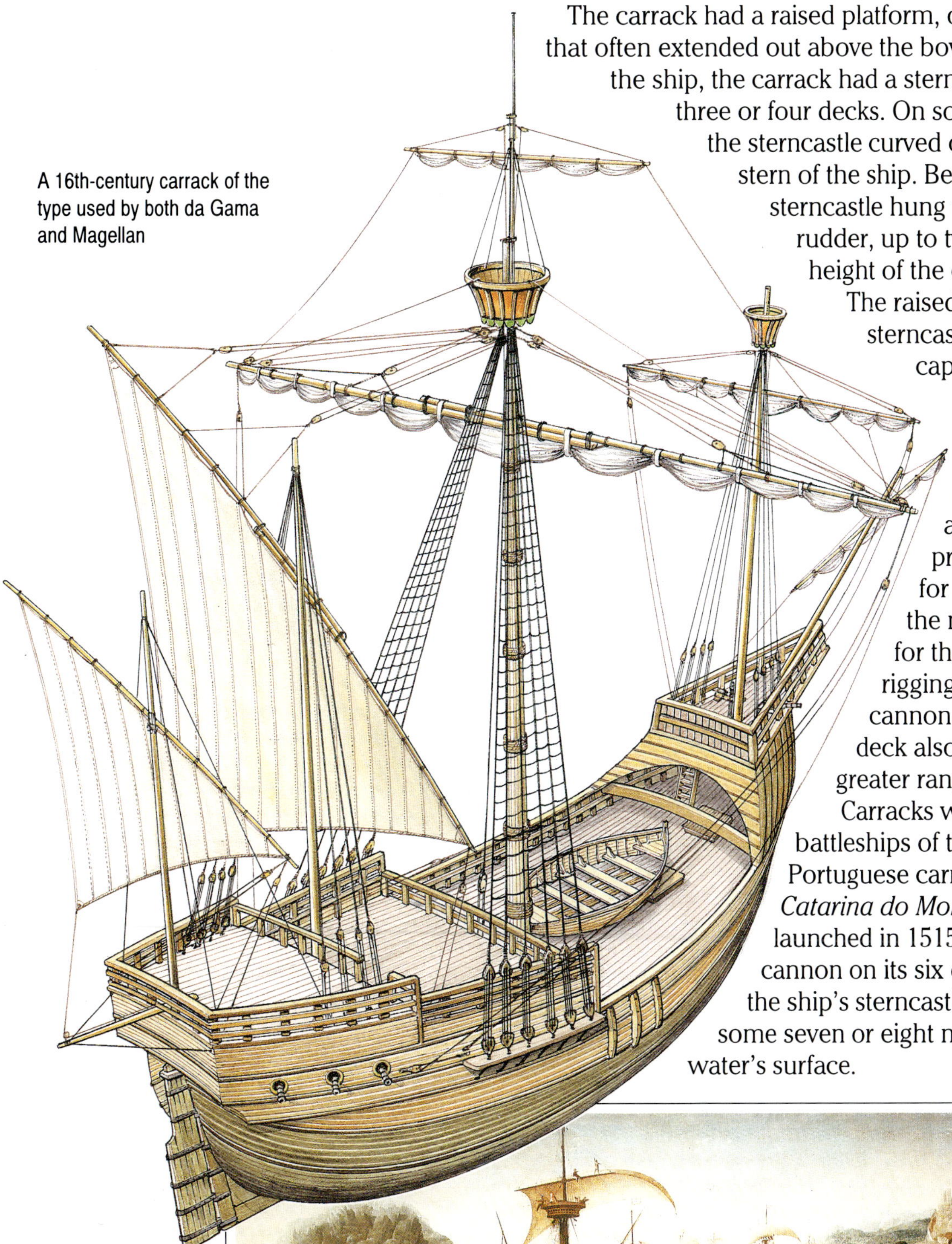

A 16th-century carrack of the type used by both da Gama and Magellan

The carrack had a raised platform, or forecastle, that often extended out above the bow. At the rear of the ship, the carrack had a sterncastle with three or four decks. On some carracks, the sterncastle curved out beyond the stern of the ship. Beneath the sterncastle hung the ship's great rudder, up to two thirds the height of the entire hull.

The raised decks of the sterncastle gave the captain a commanding viewpoint. More importantly, the additional decks provided space for cannon, leaving the main deck clear for the sails and rigging. Raising the cannon above the main deck also gave them greater range.

Carracks were used as the battleships of their day. The Portuguese carrack, the *Santa Catarina do Monte Sinai*, launched in 1515, carried 140 cannon on its six decks. At sea, the ship's sterncastle towered some seven or eight metres above the water's surface.

Portuguese carracks, painted during the first half of the 16th century. The carracks are fighting off an attack by pirates, who are using a galley powered by oars.

Da Gama's fleet

In 1497, Vasco da Gama set out with four ships under his command – two fighting carracks, the *São Gabriel* (118 tonnes) and the *São Rafael* (98 tonnes); the *Berrio* (50 tonnes and probably a caravel); and a supply ship, also a carrack. The flagship, *São Gabriel*, had a four-deck sterncastle with 14 cannon, and a three-deck forecastle with another six guns. Although he was sailing with the intention of establishing friendly trade, da Gama was obviously taking no chances. Some idea of his view of the voyage can be gained from the *padrãoes*, carved stone pillars which were carried on the supply ship. Wherever the fleet landed, da Gama intended to put up one of these *padrãoes* to prove that he, and therefore the Portuguese, had arrived there first.

Leading an expedition

Da Gama's expedition to India was the continuation of a long tradition of Portuguese exploration. During the 15th century, Portuguese sailors, armed with gunpowder weapons, had sailed along the coast of Africa offering the native African people a simple choice – trade, or suffer the consequences. So, as well as sailing to India, da Gama was also expected to set up trade deals, and to represent the king of Portugal as a diplomat.

Medical problems

By the end of the 15th century, European explorers had considerable experience of long-distance ocean voyaging. In particular, they had learned that the greatest danger, apart from storms and hurricanes, was lack of food and water. If a ship was becalmed – left drifting without wind – supplies could quickly run low.

European navigators had also learned that there were other problems besides hunger and thirst. They noticed that ships' crews often became very sick, even though they were eating and drinking regularly, but they did not understand why this happened. In fact, the crews were suffering from a disease called scurvy, caused by a lack of vitamin C in their diet. At sea, the crew lived on dry biscuits and salted meat, with none of the fresh fruit and vegetables that contain vitamin C. As a result, their gums became sore, their teeth fell out, and many eventually died.

Scurvy affected crews throughout the Age of Discovery and beyond. Not until the 18th century did the British navy discover an effective way of preventing scurvy – to issue a daily ration of lime juice, which is rich in vitamin C. This soon earned British sailors the nickname 'Limeys'.

Lime juice was issued to prevent scurvy.

Ferdinand Magellan, too, sailed as the representative of a country – Spain. But Magellan had a longer voyage as well as the harder task. He had to cope with the jealousy of his Spanish officers, who were unhappy about being under the command of a Portuguese captain. Thousands of kilometres from home, Magellan was forced to prove just how determined and ruthless an expedition leader had to be.

Magellan's fleet

In 1519, Ferdinand Magellan set sail with five ships. There were four carracks, the *San Antonio* (120 tonnes), the *Trinidad* (110 tonnes), the *Concepción* (90 tonnes), and the *Victoria* (85 tonnes); plus a caravel, the *Santiago* (75 tonnes). Magellan's flagship was the *Trinidad*, and in total he commanded some 239 officers and sailors of a dozen different nationalities, including Italians, French, Portuguese and Africans. Many of the crew were deck-hands whose main task was to haul ropes, continually adjusting the set of the sails. However, there were also numerous highly skilled specialists, such as carpenters, sailmakers, smiths, cooks, doctors, gunners, pilots (navigators) and priests. All the senior officers, except Magellan himself, were Spanish.

Equipping for voyage

Magellan took a close interest in the equipping of his fleet. As a result, a detailed list exists of what he felt to be essential equipment for the longest voyage so far undertaken.
For five ships and 239 men he took:

Navigation

24 charts: these were drawn by hand on parchment (preserved animal skin). 6 compasses: one per ship and one spare. 36 spare compass needles: the magnetized iron needle was the most important part of a compass. 21 wooden quadrants: used for measuring the angle between the sun and the horizon for navigation. 7 astrolabes: Islamic instruments used for navigation that were adopted by Europeans during the 15th century.
18 hour-glasses: instruments to measure the passage of time, which was essential for accurate navigation.

A Portuguese cannon. Similar weapons were mounted aboard carracks and other warships. On board, the wooden mounting did not have wheels.

Weapons

1000 lances: long spears that could be used for throwing or thrusting. 125 swords: these were the weapons used by the officers. 60 crossbows: the most accurate long-distance weapon of the time. 4320 crossbow bolts: 72 (six dozen) per crossbow. 120 short throwing spears and 1140 hand-thrown darts. There is no record of the total number of gunpowder weapons carried, but the smallest carrack, the *Victoria*, probably had at least 12 cannon.

Food

In addition to fresh water, which was topped up with rainwater whenever possible, the crew lived on biscuits, wine, olive oil, dried anchovies, dried pork and cheese. There were no refrigerators, so the condition of cheese after months at sea in the heat of the tropics can only be imagined. As a delicacy for the officers there was also a small amount of refined sugar, which was still an expensive luxury item at this time.

Trade

Among the goods carried for barter were: cloth, felt caps, printed handkerchiefs, combs, mirrors, brass bowls, knives, scissors, fishhooks, 250 kilograms of glass beads and some 20,000 small bells of the type attached to trained hawks and falcons. The Europeans had discovered that the African and American native peoples were very impressed by hawkbells.

Native craft

A trained hunting falcon with a hawkbell fastened to its leg.

The African people who lived on the coast usually fished the shallow waters. But it was the Arab traders who dominated the east coast of Africa, sailing their boats, called dhows, along the western shores of the Indian Ocean. From ports such as Zanzibar (off the coast of present-day Tanzania) and Mombasa (in present-day Kenya), Arab slave traders carried black slaves northwards to the Middle East and eastwards to India. When the Portuguese arrived, this sea-borne slave trade was already more than 500 years old.

In India, the design of ships was influenced by two ship types, the graceful Islamic dhows, and the dumpy Chinese ships, called junks. The triangular sails of the dhow were, however, much better suited to the winds of the Indian Ocean.

A wooden dhow being built by traditional methods in the United Arab Emirates.

Traditional outrigger canoes are still used in some parts of the Pacific Ocean.

In the South China Sea and the Pacific Ocean, both Portuguese and Spanish explorers came across outrigger craft, built by the native people. The outrigger is an ancient invention that is used to make a flat-bottomed boat more stable by adding a float on one side, or both sides, of the boat. In the Mediterranean Sea and the North Atlantic, the outrigger had long been abandoned in favour of ships with keels instead of flat bottoms. In the East, however, outriggers were still fitted to many different types of craft, from two-person canoes to boats that could hold more than 100 people.

The tall, sturdy European carracks were generally larger and more seaworthy than any of the native craft, and they impressed the local population. Some native shipbuilders began to copy European styles. This imitation is especially obvious around the Straits of Hormuz between Arabia and Iran. Soon after the Portuguese established fortresses there in the early 16th century, local shipyards began producing dhows with high, carved sterns, copying the sterns of Portuguese carracks.

The *Great Harry* was the largest and most powerful warship of its day.

Great Harry

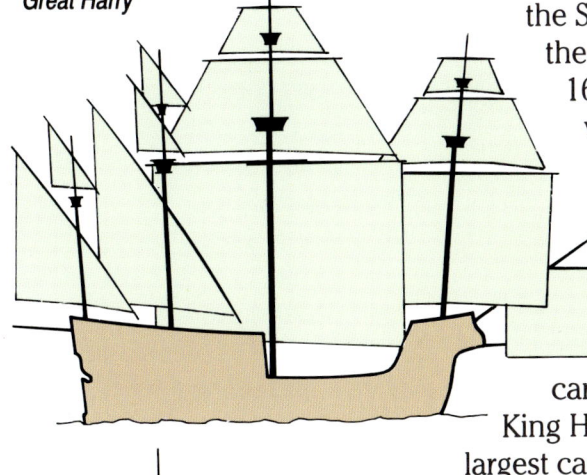

A normal-sized carrack

The age of the carrack

During the first half of the 16th century, the carrack was the most widely used European ship for trade and for warfare. As well as being useful ships, carracks also became national status symbols. In 1514, King Henry VIII of England launched the *Great Harry*, the largest carrack ever to set sail. In response, the French built *La Grande Françoise*, which was even larger – so large, in fact, that it never sailed out of port because it was too wide to fit through the mouth of the harbour.

However, the days of the carrack were numbered. By the end of the 16th century the carrack had developed into a leaner and more graceful design, the galleon. The galleon was to remain in use until the 18th century.

The voyages of Vasco da Gama

A royal send off

On 8th July 1497, da Gama's four ships sailed from the Portuguese capital, Lisbon, to try to open a sea route to India. A day or two before sailing, all the ships' officers and crew had attended a religious ceremony in the presence of the Portuguese king. The expedition was dedicated to the glory of the Catholic Church, and the men prayed for success and for protection from storms and shipwreck.

An unusual route

After leaving Lisbon, the fleet sailed southwards past the Canary Islands until they reached the Cape Verde Islands on 26th July. Here they stopped for a week while they restocked with stores and carried out minor repairs. Da Gama was now able to take advantage of another Portuguese explorer's experience of African waters. On the advice of Bartholomew Diaz, who had sailed around the southern tip of Africa in 1487-8, he turned away from the coast and set a great looping course through the South Atlantic.

Diaz had been forced to follow the African coastline because he was sailing to an unknown destination (see page 7). He found the currents along that coast extremely tricky and dangerous. For the India expedition he suggested that da Gama's fleet should stay well out at sea, where the sailing was much easier. On a map, it looks as though da Gama sailed hundreds of kilometres out of his way. In fact, by following this looping course da Gama made much better progress than if he had followed the coast.

After some 96 days in the South Atlantic, da Gama's ships finally made landfall on 7th November at St Helena Bay, just above the southern tip of Africa. The crew spent eight days mending sails, finding fresh water, and collecting firewood to use as fuel for cooking. On 16th November they put to sea again, as ready as they could be for the most perilous stage of the voyage.

Lisbon harbour in the 16th century. Large well-armed warships were essential to protect Portugal's long-distance sea trade.

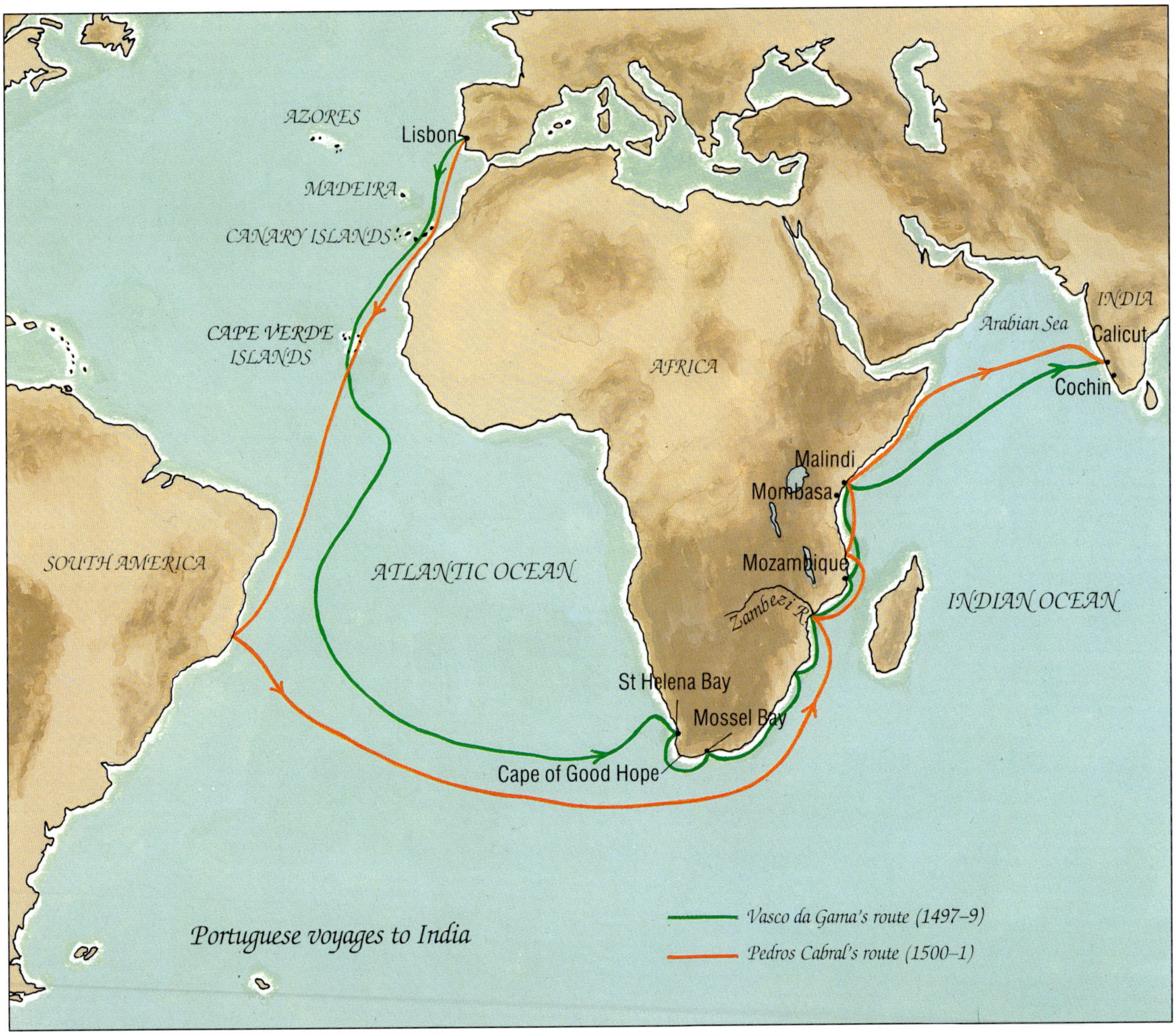

Portuguese voyages to India

— Vasco da Gama's route (1497–9)
— Pedros Cabral's route (1500–1)

Diaz had named the southern tip of Africa the 'Cape of Storms' with good reason. Rounding this Cape meant sailing through the most dangerous waters ever encountered by European sailors. Frequent storms, strong winds, swirling currents and huge waves all combined to create a deathtrap for unwary navigators.

After six days of trying to sail against winds blowing from the southwest, they finally rounded the Cape at noon on 22nd November. Three days later, they anchored at Mossel Bay where da Gama erected a stone *padrão* claiming the land for the Portuguese king. He also ordered the supply ship, which had been damaged by storms, to be broken up and its supplies and crew to be transferred to the remaining three ships.

The Cape of Good Hope

East Africa

Putting to sea once more on 8th December the fleet immediately sailed into a storm, and for three weeks the ships were buffeted by winds and currents. Eventually, on Christmas Day 1497, they were able to anchor off the coast of Natal. Ahead of them lay the coastline of East Africa, as yet unexplored by Europeans; and somewhere over the ocean lay India and the Spice Islands.

Da Gama sailed northwards along the coast until his fleet reached the mouth of the Zambezi River (named the 'River of Good Signs' by the Portuguese) on 25th January. Here, da Gama erected another *padrão*, and the ships' crews rested for a month.

To India

The fleet continued up the coast, passing the port of Mombasa on 7th April 1498. A week later they anchored at Malindi, a major port for trade between Africa and India. At Malindi, da Gama was able to find a local pilot who agreed to guide the fleet across the Arabian Sea.

After a further 23 days at sea, the lookouts sighted the Ghat Mountains on the horizon, and on 20th May the fleet anchored off Calicut, the main trading centre for the whole of southern India. Da Gama insisted on erecting a *padrão*, but its meaning does not seem to have been understood by the local inhabitants. The Hindu zamorin (ruler) of Calicut welcomed the Portuguese with great courtesy and ceremony.

Da Gama was, however, unable to make an agreement about trade with the zamorin. The Islamic merchants in Calicut wanted to keep control over the valuable spice trade, and they persuaded the zamorin that it was unwise to do business directly with the European Christians. Da Gama left Calicut empty-handed except for six Hindu scholars, whom he took back to Portugal.

Homeward bound

Da Gama decided to return to Europe in August 1498. Unfortunately, late summer was the wrong season to sail westwards across the Arabian Sea, and the winds were against him. The crossing took nearly five times as long as the outward trip, and many of the crew died of scurvy.

When the fleet eventually reached Malindi on the African coast, da Gama had no alternative but to order the *São Rafael* to be abandoned and burned. There simply were not enough sailors to provide crew for three ships. The remaining two ships rounded the Cape together in March the following year. Sailing aboard the *São Gabriel*, da Gama finally returned to Lisbon on 9th September 1499, where he was given a hero's welcome. In response to the good news brought by da Gama, the Portuguese king renamed the Cape of Storms the Cape of Good Hope.

The *padrão* erected by da Gama near Malindi on the East African coast.

Success and disaster

The Portuguese were expecting da Gama's voyage to be a success and a second, larger expedition was already being prepared. In March 1500, Pedros Cabral sailed from Lisbon with a fleet of 13 ships. Cabral followed da Gama's route to the Cape Verde Islands, but then took an even longer westward loop through the South Atlantic. Cabral travelled so far west that his first landfall (on 22nd April) was Brazil, in South America. After claiming Brazil for Portugal and naming it the 'Land of the True Cross', Cabral sailed on to India.

The Brazilian coast, sighted by Cabral on his way to India

His looping course took him well south of the Cape of Good Hope, and his fleet did not make landfall again until the ships anchored in the Zambezi River. From here, Cabral sailed up the coast and then across to India. At Calicut, he succeeded in establishing a Portuguese 'factory' – a place where trade goods were stored.

Cabral departed for Portugal believing his mission to have been a success. But after he left there was a riot in which the factory was burned, and the Portuguese staff were killed. When news of the killings at Calicut reached Lisbon, the king ordered immediate revenge. Da Gama demanded to be allowed to lead this expedition and he was given command of a fleet of some 20 warships.

The outward journey passed without trouble, and da Gama anchored off Calicut in the early summer of 1502. His orders were clear: he was to avenge the murdered Portuguese citizens, and he was to make sure that the local inhabitants understood that Portuguese authority was backed by force.

The Monument of the Discoveries in Lisbon juts out into the River Tagus. Prince Henry the Navigator stands, caravel in hand, at its tip, with da Gama and many other Portuguese explorers behind.

From their offshore anchorage, da Gama's ships bombarded Calicut with cannon fire, destroying all the large buildings within range and starting many fires. When the zamorin sent out a fleet of 200 local ships to attack the Europeans, the Portuguese gunners destroyed them with their cannon fire.

Da Gama then sailed down the coast to Calicut's rival port, Cochin, where he made a trade treaty with the local ruler. Da Gama returned to Portugal in triumph for a second time, his flagship laden with spices, gold and other precious gifts.

After this voyage he went into retirement, although he continued to advise the king on matters relating to India. In 1524 he was appointed the Portuguese viceroy (ruler) of India. He made a final voyage to the East, but died at Cochin soon after his arrival.

Local cultures - Africa and India

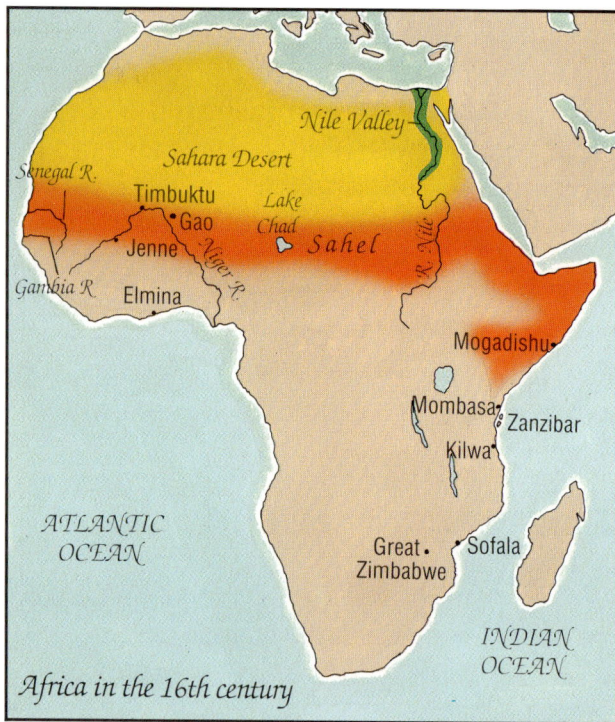

Africa in the 16th century

Da Gama's voyage around Africa to India provided Europe with valuable new knowledge and experience. But da Gama knew little about the countries to which he had travelled, except that they were sources of gold, spices and other riches. This chapter looks at the history of Africa and India before the arrival of the Portuguese.

Africa

The continent of Africa can be divided into two regions separated by the Sahara Desert. North of the Sahara, a narrow coastal strip (including the fertile Nile Valley) had long been a part of the Mediterranean world. The countries of North Africa were included in the territory of the Roman Empire and had later been conquered by the Islamic Empire. South of the natural barrier formed by the Sahara desert, Africa had remained fairly isolated from the rest of the world. The vast majority of the sub-Saharan native Africans worshipped their own gods and followed their own cultures.

Islam had been introduced into Africa in two areas. South of the Sahara lies a belt of land known as the Sahel. Since before the days of the Roman Empire, camel caravans had traded across the Sahara between the Sahel and the Mediterranean. Gold, slaves and salt from the interior of Africa were exchanged for food and manufactured goods from the Mediterranean. As a result of this trade, oasis towns such as Timbuktu had become

Timbuktu is in the middle of the Sahara Desert. The city is surrounded by irrigated fields.

The Portuguese fort of São Jorge at Elmina. A series of forts along the African coast provided the Portuguese with storage for trade goods, including slaves.

rich and important. When Islam spread across North Africa during the 7th and 8th centuries, it soon found its way across the desert with the traders.

In East Africa, Islamic influence arrived by sea, on dhows sailing southwards from the Arabian Gulf. By the end of the 9th century, Arab merchants had established trading posts as far south as Zanzibar. At first the trade consisted of African gold and ivory exchanged for Islamic pottery. By the 12th century this had developed into a busy trade between Africa, Arabia and India.

The Portuguese

In the 15th century, thanks to the Papal Treaty of 1479 (see page 9), Portugal was the only European country permitted to trade with sub-Saharan Africa. Other European states could send ships to Africa only with Portugal's permission. However, this did not prevent other European sailors from attempting to trade with Africa. They called themselves merchant-adventurers, but the Portuguese called them pirates and thieves.

In order to protect their trading rights, the Portuguese built a series of forts along the African coast. The first of these, the castle of São Jorge, was built in 1482 at Elmina on the coast of present-day Ghana. By 1500, Portuguese influence had extended to East Africa, and forts had been built at Sofala and Kilwa (in present-day Mozambique). Later, forts were built further north at Zanzibar and Mombasa (see page 10).

A pottery head made by the Nok people

West African states

By the time the Portuguese arrived in the mid 15th century, the native peoples of West Africa had already become organised into a number of independent states. Some of these were no more than local chiefdoms; while others developed into large trading empires that lasted for several centuries. Little is known about these African states, because none of them had a written language. However, by studying tools and other artefacts, modern archaeologists have been able to piece together some of the early history of Africa.

Iron-working was discovered in West Africa, some time before 500 BC. Early iron-working was developed independently by cultures such as that of the Nok people. The Nok people lived in the area which is present-day northern Nigeria. Nok culture was at its height between 400 BC and 300 AD.

Some time around 500 AD, the first towns were built in sub-Saharan Africa. The most important of these were Jenne and

The market in Jenne. In the background is a mosque built of mud bricks in the local style.

Gao, situated inland on the Niger River. As the towns in this region grew in number and size, trade between them increased. By around 1200, many of the towns had become incorporated into the empire of Mali. Stretching inland from between the mouths of the Senegal and Gambia rivers, the empire of Mali eventually extended to include desert trading towns such as Timbuktu. Further inland, around Lake Chad, was the smaller empire of Kanem. However, by the end of the 15th century, the empires of Mali and Kanem had both been absorbed into the much larger Songhay Empire, which was governed from Gao.

Forest kingdoms

Mali, Kanem and Songhay were all trading empires that took advantage of the easy travel over the grasslands of the Sahel. Further south, among the tropical rainforests, other cultures had developed that were of far greater interest to the Portuguese.

The state of Akan (present-day Ghana) was the source of most of West Africa's golden wealth. Akan gold was obtained from rivers inland and transported down to the coast. The Portuguese soon learned that the best way to trade for Akan gold was with slaves captured elsewhere on the African coast. The importance of Akan is shown by the fact that the Portuguese built no less than five permanent settlements along its short coastline.

Further east, in present-day Nigeria, the peoples of Benin had established themselves as the most important slave traders in the region, trading both with the Songhay Empire and Akan. When the Portuguese arrived, the Benin chiefs were delighted to welcome new customers.

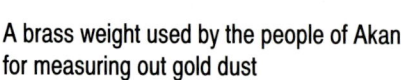

A brass weight used by the people of Akan for measuring out gold dust

East Africa

In East Africa, the situation was quite different. The Indian Ocean sea trade meant that ports grew up along the coast. During the first half of the 16th century the Portuguese took over as the most important sea power in the area, and Portuguese forts replaced the Arab ports as the centres of trade. Only the northernmost of the Arab ports, Mogadishu (in present-day Somalia), remained under Islamic influence.

The stone ruins of Great Zimbabwe

Little is known of the peoples of East Africa further inland at this time. The only state that attracted the attention of the Portuguese was the kingdom of Monomotapa, situated around the upper part of the Zambezi River. Monomotapa was the major source of gold in East Africa, and throughout the 16th century a series of Portuguese expeditions tried to find and capture its gold mines. In 1522, one of these expeditions discovered the ruins of a large city called Great Zimbabwe, which are still standing today. Although we do not know exactly when Great Zimbabwe was built, or who built it, the massive stone walls remain as a striking monument to the achievements of the native African peoples.

India

For the Portuguese, India was a complete contrast to Africa. Instead of bartering with tribal chiefs, the Portuguese found themselves dealing with the people of a sophisticated civilisation that was far older than their own. Indians had been living in cities with paved streets and drains when the largest settlement in Portugal was a cluster of thatched huts. Although India had been invaded many times over the centuries, the essentials of Indian culture had remained largely unchanged for about 3000 years before the Portuguese arrived.

Today, the Indian subcontinent is divided into three countries: India, Pakistan and Bangladesh. This division is the result of 20th-century politics. At the time of Vasco da Gama, the whole of the subcontinent was one country – India.

Mohenjo-Daro, one of the Indus Valley cities, built of sun-dried bricks nearly 5000 years ago

Cities and religions

The first Indian cities were built around 2500BC along the valley of the Indus River in northwestern India (present-day Pakistan). These cities were well-planned, and were laid out in a grid pattern, with underground drains running beneath each street. Although

A Buddhist monk standing in front of a statue of the Buddha

little is known about the people who built these cities, archaeologists have discovered evidence of trade between India and the Middle East at this time.

Around 1500BC, the Indus Valley cities declined, possibly as a result of invasions from the northwest. India then entered the Vedic period, so called because the sacred *Vedas* (hymns) of the Hindu religion were composed and written down during this time. The centre of Indian civilisation shifted eastwards to the banks of the Ganges River, but slowly broke up as different tribes fought amongst themselves. The final collapse of Vedic civilisation was around 600BC. During the following century, two great teachers appeared who criticised Hindu values. Both founded a new religion.

Gautama Siddhartha, the Buddha, (563-483BC) was the most influential of the two. He taught that through many stages of self-improvement, during which greed and hatred are destroyed, a person can reach a state of *nirvana* (absolute peace). Buddhism soon spread throughout India, and beyond to China and Southeast Asia.

Vardhamana 'Jina' (540-468BC) taught that freedom from the sufferings of the world could only be obtained through fasting and self-punishment. His followers called themselves Jains ('of Jina'), but the religion did not spread beyond Central India.

Invasions and empires

In 272BC, an Indian prince named Asoka founded the Mauryan Empire, the first and largest of all the Indian empires. From his

A stone carving from the Gupta Empire

Hinduism

The Hindu religion developed over thousands of years, and is today the main religion in India. It has a number of different gods, each with several names depending on which side of their character they are showing. Hindus believe that, after death, the soul is reborn.

Traditional Hindu society was divided into lots of classes, known as castes. A person could not change caste during his or her lifetime, but by living a good life he or she could be reborn into a better caste.

The ruler's palace in Jaipur. This Islamic-style architecture was brought to India by invaders from the north.

family homeland in eastern India, Asoka conquered most of the subcontinent except the southernmost tip. Asoka had been brought up as a Hindu, but he was horrified by the cruelty of warfare and converted to the peace-loving teachings of Buddhism. He became known as the 'prince of peace', and he made a point of establishing fair laws.

After Asoka's death in 232BC, his empire quickly declined. Eventually the Kushans, who originally came from the northwestern borders of China, established a new empire across northern India that lasted from about 50AD to 250AD. During the Kushan Empire, there was considerable trade between India and the Roman Empire. Roman ships even visited trading ports in southern India and Ceylon (present-day Sri Lanka).

After the collapse of the Kushans, northern India was united once again under local Hindu rulers, the Guptas. The Gupta Empire lasted from about 320AD to 530AD, and produced some of the finest Indian art. During the 6th century, the Gupta Empire broke up into a number of small Hindu kingdoms. By 700AD, the importance of Buddhism had declined in India, although Buddhism continued to flourish in China, Korea and elsewhere.

The arrival of Islam

In 712AD a small area of northwest India (around present-day Karachi in Pakistan) was invaded by Arabs and claimed as part of the newly established Islamic Empire. For the next 300 years, the Hindu rulers of India were able to withstand the forces of Islam. However, during the 12th century Islamic invaders gradually conquered much of northern India. In 1206, they overthrew the ruler of Delhi and established the Islamic Sultanate of Delhi. By the end of the 14th century, the Sultanate of Delhi extended across the whole of north and central India. The Islamic rulers tolerated Hinduism, but they would not accept Buddhism. As a result, Buddhist temples and sacred writings were destroyed, and Buddhists were driven out of the Sultanate.

The south of India remained free of Islamic control, and was dominated by the independent Hindu state of Vijayanagar. However, the Hindu rulers were unable to prevent Islamic merchants from establishing themselves in southern Indian ports. Since the 9th century Arab merchants had traded with India, and they had slowly taken control of the Indian Ocean spice trade. This control was finally threatened by the arrival of Vasco da Gama and the Portuguese fleet.

Horizons

You could find out about these people who ruled in different parts of the world in the 14th, 15th and 16th centuries: the Ming emperors (in China); the Shoguns (in Japan); Suleiman the Magnificent (the sultan of the Turkish Ottoman Empire); Timur the Lame, or Tamerlane (Mongol emperor in Central Asia); Montezuma (Aztec emperor in Central America).

The voyage of Ferdinand Magellan

Charles V, king of Spain and Holy Roman Emperor (right), who financed and supported Magellan's expedition

'Rights of rope and knife'

Ferdinand Magellan was an orphan, and while still young he was sent to work as a page at the Portuguese court. When he was older he served as an officer in the Portuguese navy, fought battles in India, and supervised the building of fortresses in Africa. In 1514, he quarrelled with the king and left Portugal. In 1517 he went to work for the Spanish.

Magellan had a dream: to do what Columbus had failed to do and to sail westwards to reach India. Since the discovery of Brazil, there had been rumours about the existence of a sea passage around the bottom of South America that led to another ocean, and to India. Magellan was determined to find this sea passage.

His proposals were very attractive to the Spanish. Columbus had discovered America for Spain, but America had few spices. At that time, spices were grown mainly in India and the Spice Islands. The Portuguese had control over the spice trade with India, and had made direct contact with the Spice Islands, although they did not control the trade there. The Spanish were jealous of Portugal's success and they seized the chance offered by Magellan to find a new sea route to the Spice Islands.

In September 1519 the Armada (fleet) of the Spice Islands, five small wooden ships, set sail from the Spanish port of Sanlúcar. Although most of the officers were Spanish, the fleet was under

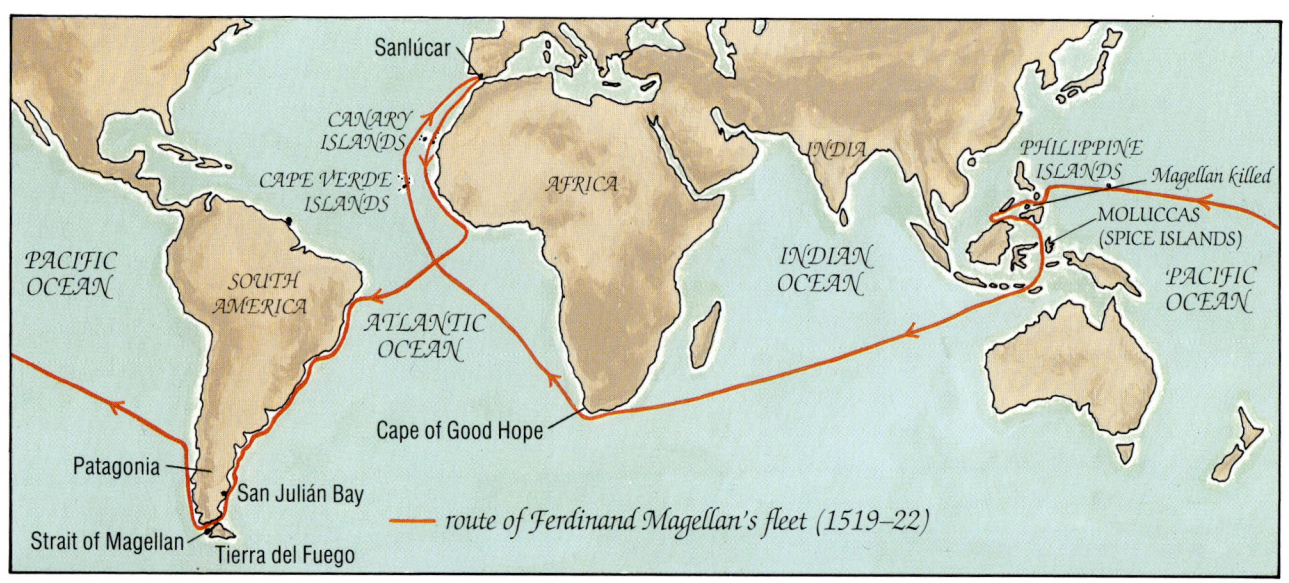

the command of the foreigner, Ferdinand Magellan. The king of Spain had given Magellan absolute power of life and death – 'rights of rope and knife' – over the entire fleet.

Daggers at midnight

Magellan's fleet sailed south to the Canary Islands, where the ships took on fresh food and water, and along the coast of Africa, avoiding Portuguese patrol ships. Magellan then turned westwards and crossed the Atlantic, making landfall on the Brazilian coast. From here he sailed southwards once more, making slow progress because every inlet had to be explored in case it proved to be the way through to India. By the end of March 1520, the fleet had reached the bay of San Julián in what is now Argentina; no Europeans had ever sailed so far south before. Magellan decided to spend the winter at anchor there. (In the southern hemisphere winter runs from April to September.)

A picture of Ferdinand Magellan which appeared in 1673. He is holding a pair of dividers, used to measure distances on charts.

The Spanish officers did not trust their Portuguese leader. On the first day of April, Magellan invited all his senior officers to dine with him aboard the *Trinidad*. None of them came, and later they sent a demand that the fleet return to Spain. This was mutiny!

Magellan acted swiftly and ruthlessly. He sent a messenger to the *Victoria*, to demand that the captain report to Magellan immediately. The Spanish captain laughed when he heard the message. Acting on Magellan's orders, the messenger immediately drew a dagger and stabbed the captain in the throat, killing him. Boatloads of sailors loyal to Magellan took over two of the other ships, and a third surrendered after being hit by cannon fire from the *Trinidad*. By daybreak on 2nd April, Magellan had regained control of his fleet. Some of the ringleaders of the mutiny were put in chains, others were stranded ashore and left to fend for themselves.

The Strait of Magellan

In September, at the beginning of the southern spring, the fleet sailed southwards once more. On 21st October, when they were nearer the South Pole than the equator, they sighted a promising inlet. As they sailed westwards along the inlet, Magellan sent one or two of his ships ahead as scouts. One day the *San Antonio* did not return. The ship's officers and crew had mutinied again, and they sailed back to Spain where they spread lies about Magellan.

Not knowing the true fate of the *San Antonio*, Magellan sailed slowly on, sometimes beneath sheer, towering cliffs. Even during summer the weather was dreadful, with sudden storms and huge

A 16th-century map showing the newly discovered Strait of Magellan. The South American mainland is shown to be populated by hostile tribes. The fact that the discovery was Spanish is emphasised by the Spanish ships on either side of the Strait.

The Strait of Magellan

waves. Eventually, on 28th November, the fleet sailed out into a vast glittering ocean. Although he was not the first European to see this ocean (Balboa did that in 1513 when he crossed Central America on foot), Magellan did give it a name. Balboa had merely called it the 'Great South Sea'. Magellan named it the Pacific Ocean because he found gentle (pacific) winds there. The narrow passage between the Atlantic and the Pacific oceans was afterwards named the Strait of Magellan in his honour.

For a short while, the fleet sailed northwards along the west coast of South America. Magellan then headed out across the Pacific Ocean. For 98 or 99 days (the exact number is uncertain), Magellan's ships sailed northeast across the Pacific without making landfall. They passed one or two small islands, but did not stop because of the danger of becoming grounded on a reef.

After more than three months without fresh food or water, the crews were in a terrible state. The ship's biscuits had become rotten, and the drinking water was so foul that sailors held their

Islands and a coral reef in the Pacific Ocean. Magellan and his crew passed several small islands, but they could not stop because of the danger of running aground on reefs.

noses while they drank. At one point, rats were being sold for food – two for a gold coin for those who could afford such luxuries. The poorer sailors were reduced to chewing on old leather mats. Some of the crew survived by eating flying fish that occasionally leapt over the side and fell on to the decks.

Altogether, at least 29 of the crew died of starvation and disease, and about another 30 became so ill that they could not work or even move. Scurvy (see page 14) was the worst of the diseases aboard the ships. Without fresh fruit and vegetables, many of the victims died after weeks of sickness.

Pacific islands

At last, a lookout sighted a lush green island. Ashore, the starving sailors found coconuts, bananas, sugar cane and yams; and the offshore reef was teeming with fat fish. They were saved! After a voyage from the bay of San Julián of nearly 15,000 kilometres, they had reached the island of Guam. Magellan had completed

Utamac Bay, the landing site of Magellan on the island of Guam. (Inset) Two members of Magellan's crew try out a native canoe around the island of Guam.

the longest voyage without a stop that any European had so far made. Although he was relieved still to be alive, Magellan was deeply disappointed. The route across the Pacific was far too long to be practical, and far too difficult ever to rival the Portuguese route to the Spice Islands. In addition, the native inhabitants of the island were friendly but did not seem to be rich. In fact, they had a habit of stealing anything that they could lay their hands on. Magellan named the island 'Ladrones' (Island of Thieves), and burned down a village to set an example. He then sailed westwards.

A week of smooth sailing brought the fleet to the outermost of the Philippine Islands. Anchoring offshore, Magellan put some of the sickest sailors ashore to recover from their illnesses. The local inhabitants were very helpful and gifts were exchanged. In return for hawkbells and mirrors, Magellan was presented with a basket of ginger and a bar of gold. His mood improved considerably as he realised that the presence of gold and ginger meant that India and the Spice Islands must be nearby.

Continuing westwards, the fleet arrived at the island of Cebu. Here, Magellan allowed himself to celebrate. By his calculations, they were now west of the Spice Islands; they had proved that it was possible to reach the East by sailing westwards from Europe. They had also proved beyond any possible doubt that the world was round, that all the oceans were linked, and that the continents were, in fact, just huge islands.

Ginger root: the plant grows up to one metre tall, but only the root is used as a spice.

The battle on the beach

Magellan and his crew were given a very warm welcome by the inhabitants of Cebu. When Magellan claimed the island for Spain, the local chief readily agreed. When Magellan suggested that the chief become a Christian (to set an example to the other natives), he also agreed. What Magellan did not realise was that the ruler was merely being polite to his strange guests, as was the custom among the islanders.

Later, the chief sent a message saying that Cilapulapu, the ruler of the nearby island of Mactan, was refusing to acknowledge the authority of the king of Spain. In fact the chief was trying to use the Spanish to defeat one of his local enemies. On 27th April, Magellan set out to subdue Cilapulapu with a party of 60 armed men in three rowing boats. As soon as they landed, they attacked Cilapulapu's village and were met by hundreds of hostile natives.

For several hours both sides fired arrows and threw spears at each other. Eventually Magellan decided to retreat to the boats. The natives closed in, and Magellan was hit in the face by a spear. His men tried to rescue him, but could not. In seconds, his body had been hacked into pieces. The survivors hurried back to Cebu with the sad news.

A perilous return

The remaining officers decided to take the two best ships, the *Trinidad* and the *Victoria*, and sail southwards to the Spice Islands. A journey that should have taken them a week lasted three months, and they finally arrived on 8th November 1521.

Gratefully the crew filled the holds with cloves bartered from the natives. If they could manage to take these back to Spain, then the voyage would have been worthwhile. After leaving the Spice Islands they sailed well to the south to avoid Portuguese patrols because they were now carrying an illegal cargo of cloves.

The *Trinidad* soon sprang a leak, and the *Victoria* sailed on alone. Conditions aboard worsened as the weeks passed, and more sailors became ill and died. The *Victoria* successfully rounded the Cape of Good Hope, and sailed northwards to the Cape Verde Islands. Here, the Portuguese governor discovered the cargo of cloves. He seized 13 of the crew, but the rest managed to escape. Eventually, on 6th September 1522, the *Victoria*, commanded by Captain Juan de Elcano, arrived in Spain after a voyage lasting almost three years.

The Spanish authorities were very pleased to receive the cloves, but the crew got little thanks. The lies spread by the mutineers on the *San Antonio* had seriously damaged Magellan's reputation, and he was considered a criminal. Magellan only achieved his deserved fame much later, when historians began to piece together the story of world exploration.

A clove tree. The flower buds are dried to form the spice cloves.

This fabric, made in Sumatra, Indonesia, commemorates the arrival of the first European ships on the Sumatran coast. The *Trinidad* and the *Victoria* sailed through the Indonesian islands on their journey home.

Local cultures - Patagonia and the Pacific

The land of big feet

Magellan's crews spent very little time on the tropical coast of Brazil, just enough to take on fresh water and food after their Atlantic crossing. Instead, they continued southwards until they reached the land they called Patagonia.

Patagonia is the southernmost region of the South American continent. Apart from the Andes Mountains in the west, it is a flat, dry, windswept place. The Spanish fleet remained at anchor in the bay of San Julián throughout the winter, and the strong winds and freezing temperatures did not encourage them to explore far inland. Even so, they did make contact with some of the local inhabitants.

Little is known about the pre-European population of this region, because there are few traces of their existence for archaeologists to study. The Spanish sailors believed that the natives had remarkably big feet, and named them Los Patagones

The coastline of Patagonia, Argentina

Magellanic penguins

The South American rhea is a relative of the ostrich.

('the people with big feet'). This unusual appearance was probably because the natives wrapped their feet in large bundles of dry grass to protect them from the frozen ground. Although the natives grew some crops they were also skilful hunters. Their favourite prey was the rhea (a large flightless bird like an ostrich). Rheas could run faster than human hunters, but could be brought down by throwing a bolas. The bolas was a pair of tennis ball-sized stones, tied together with cords made of tightly plaited dried grass which, when thrown, tangled themselves around the rhea's legs and feet.

Sailing through the stormy Strait of Magellan the following spring, the fleet was unable to put in to land. Nevertheless, some members of the expedition probably became the first Europeans to see penguins, which are found only in the southern hemisphere. One South American species was later named the Magellanic penguin. The crews also sighted some of the many volcanoes that give the island to the south of the Strait its name – Tierra del Fuego (Land of Fire).

Filipino culture

The Philippine Islands had been invaded from the sea several times before the Spanish arrived, and the inhabitants had inherited a wide variety of cultural and religious influences. The

The people of the Pacific

As the Spanish ships voyaged across the Pacific, they unknowingly sailed through the vast oceanic territory of the Polynesians. Setting out from the Philippines around 1500BC, the Polynesians had gradually colonised nearly all of the Pacific Islands. By 1000AD they had introduced new crops and livestock over a huge area of the Pacific Ocean and had established hundreds of permanent settlements.

The Polynesians were the greatest navigators the world has ever known. Travelling in small open boats, they established themselves in a region where only one per cent of the surface area is land; the rest being open sea. The basic Polynesian craft was the outrigger canoe (see page 17) fitted with a small sail of woven palm leaves. Although some canoes carried up to 100 people, most were much smaller, carrying 20 people at most. Using these tiny craft, the Polynesians travelled the thousands of kilometres between their islands. Polynesian navigators used primitive charts made of seashells linked by sticks bound together with dried grass. The shells represented islands, and the sticks represented winds and currents. Similar charts are still used on remote islands today.

first arrivals were probably a dark-skinned people, quite similar to the Aborigines of Australia. Over the centuries, settlers also came from Indonesia, Vietnam and the Malay Peninsula. By 2000BC, the population was already very mixed. The Polynesians, whose direct ancestors are still a mystery, used the Philippines as a starting point for their colonisation of the Pacific. Later arrivals in the Philippines, between 500BC and 500AD, brought with them the Hindu and Buddhist religions from India.

Regular sea trade with southern China was established by around 800AD, and shortly afterwards the first Islamic merchants arrived from Arabia by way of India. By the time of Magellan's arrival, Filipino culture (the word Filipino is used when referring to the people of the Philippines) had already become thoroughly mixed.

The Spice Islands

Both the Portuguese and Spanish expeditions set out to sail to the Spice Islands. Today, these islands are known as the Moluccas, but in Magellan's day they were named for their most famous product – spice. At this time, some spices grew nowhere else in the world but on these islands; and the whole of the

The Moluccas, Indonesia: in the 16th century the forests of the Spice Islands provided nearly the whole world's supply of exotic spices.

annual supply – for India, Asia and Europe – was grown and harvested there.

The natural vegetation of the Moluccas is tropical rainforest, fringed with mangrove swamps along the coast. Among the thousands of exotic plants growing in the rainforest are two that are extremely valuable – cloves and nutmeg.

Cloves are the dried flower buds of a species of tropical myrtle (an evergreen shrub). Picked when green, the buds are dried in the sun to concentrate the sticky oil that gives them their particular flavour. The pure oil, pressed from the dried buds, was used in medicine (and is still used today to provide relief from toothache). Cloves were also added to stews, roast meats, desserts, cakes and heated wine, where they provided a warm, spicy flavour that became especially popular in Europe.

Nutmeg comes from the fruit (known as a nutmeg-apple) of a rainforest tree. Nutmeg itself is the dried seed found at the centre of the nutmeg-apple. Mace, another popular spice, is obtained from the dried outer covering of the fruit. Nutmeg and mace were both widely used in medicine and cooking. Other spices obtained from different tropical trees were often called nutmeg, for example Jamaican nutmeg and Brazilian nutmeg, but the true nutmeg grows wild only in the Moluccas and parts of New Guinea.

Since before the days of the Roman Empire, Europeans had used spices imported from the Moluccas, but they did not know where they came from until the beginning of the 16th century. Marco Polo believed that he had discovered the source of the spices, but the islands of Java and Sumatra which he named did not produce their own spices; they, too, imported them from the Moluccas and then exported them on to India.

After the visit made in 1521 by the survivors of Magellan's expedition, the Spice Islands were claimed by Spain under the terms of the same treaty that had granted them the rights to America (see page 11). This claim was allowed, but in 1528 Spain sold its interest in the Spice Islands to Portugal. At this time, the Spanish government was busy with the conquest of Central America, and did not have enough money to finance voyages into the Pacific. As a result the Portuguese were to enjoy complete control over the trade in the valuable products of the Spice Islands for the next 50 years.

Nutmegs being dried in a loft in the Moluccas, Indonesia

A ripe nutmeg with red mace surrounding the fruit

What happened later

Colonial apartments in Macao

The achievements of both da Gama and Magellan were outstanding. Da Gama proved that long-distance sea trade was practical, and Magellan proved that the world was round, and that the oceans were connected together. By 1550, Spanish and Portuguese warships ruled the waves, and very nearly the whole of the world as it was known to the Europeans.

The Portuguese empire

Da Gama's triumphant return to Lisbon in 1499 was a just reward to Portugal for almost a century of exploration by sea. Within 50 years, Portugal changed from a small kingdom on the fringe of European affairs to the centre of a worldwide empire. In 1510, the Portuguese conquered the territory of Goa in western India after a fierce battle with Islamic forces. Goa gave the Portuguese a large permanent base in the East, and from here they extended their influence. By 1530, they had also established smaller bases at Bombay to the north, and in Ceylon (Sri Lanka) to the south. Portuguese ships first reached China in 1517 and began regular

Mercantile capitalism

The voyages of da Gama and Magellan were part of a new European attitude to the world. Up to the 15th century, Europeans had been content simply to import exotic Eastern goods. Silks and spices had arrived in the eastern Mediterranean from Islamic ports such as Istanbul in Turkey, and Alexandria in Egypt. However, during the 15th century the new economic philosophy of mercantile capitalism had developed. In simple terms, the argument of this new philosophy was that instead of buying Eastern goods that were supplied by foreigners, Europeans should own both the source of the goods and the means to transport them to Europe. In this way all the profits would stay in European hands, rather than being lost to Eastern merchants and Islamic ship owners.

European merchants of the 16th century count the profits from a successful voyage. Their connection with overseas trade (Africa or the New World) is shown by the parrot sitting behind them.

trade with the port of Canton. Some 40 years later, they established a larger settlement at nearby Macao.

This Eastern trading empire brought great wealth to Portugal. The supply of spices to Europe was no longer threatened by disturbances within the Islamic Empire, or by Mediterranean warfare with the Ottoman Turks. As a result, the demand for spices increased. The Lisbon spice market became the financial centre of Europe, and huge profits were made.

Spanish concerns

The situation in Spain was quite different. America was undoubtedly a valuable prize, but its true value had still to be revealed. The conquest of Mexico had only just begun when Magellan sailed, and the riches of Peru were still a distant rumour. Not surprisingly, Magellan's voyage was not considered a success, despite the cargo of cloves brought home by the survivors. The route was far too long to be practical for trade, and the costs were huge. Three out of five ships had been lost, and fewer than one in ten of the sailors had returned to Spain alive.

But the 16th century was to be Spain's century. The rise in Spain's fortunes began in 1492, when the last of the Islamic invaders was finally driven out of the country. In 1519, the Spanish king, Charles V (see page 28), was elected emperor of the Holy Roman Empire (roughly the same area as present-day Germany), and this gave him tremendous power in Europe. By waging war against France, he was able to strengthen Spain's control over its territories in Italy and the Netherlands.

In America, Spanish soldiers captured the capital of the Aztec Empire (present-day Mexico City) in 1520. By 1533 they had completed the conquest of the South American empire of the Incas. Huge amounts of looted American gold was shipped back to Spain. This was followed by a seemingly endless supply of silver from the mines in Bolivia. After the looting had ended, Spain once again remembered the Pacific Ocean. Interest in a sea route from Europe to the western side of America was now renewed because America could be used as a starting-point for voyages to the Philippine Islands (named after Philip II of Spain, son of Charles V).

In 1569, an armed force was sent to the Philippines to claim the islands for Spain. After some skirmishes with the Portuguese, Spanish troops landed on the island of Panay and established their headquarters at a town called

Philip II of Spain

The modern city of Manila still reveals Spanish influence (inset: the cathedral in the historic old quarter).

Manila. Within five years, almost all of the Philippine Islands had been conquered by Spain.

In 1571, the Spanish fleet, helped by the ships from Venice and other Italian states defeated the Ottoman Turks at the Mediterranean sea battle of Lepanto. The Spanish king was acclaimed as the saviour of Christian Europe. Then, after the conquest of the Philippine Islands, Philip laid claim to the Portuguese throne. The kingdoms of Spain and Portugal were united in 1580. Spanish power was now at its height, with control over an empire made up of nearly all the overseas territories conquered by Europe. However, this situation was not to last. Even as the Spanish Empire was completed, its supremacy was being challenged.

The Dutch revolt

Spanish troubles began in the 1560s when the inhabitants of the Netherlands rebelled against Spanish rule. In 1581, the rebels (who called themselves the Dutch) declared the independence of their country, which they named the United Provinces.

Neither side could make much progress on land, but the Dutch attacked the Spanish on the seas, too. Dutch sailors had plenty of experience in the stormy waters of the North Sea and North Atlantic Ocean. Following the routes established by Portuguese and Spanish navigators, the Dutch had no difficulty in sending ships to the Indian and Pacific oceans, where they raided enemy ships and settlements. By the end of the 16th century, the Dutch had captured some of the smaller Portuguese forts. This was the beginning of a future Dutch Empire. During the next century, the Dutch would become a major power in the East.

Spain defeated

The Dutch rebels were Protestants, and they were helped by the Protestant nation of England. The English were not allies of Spain or France, and were delighted to make mischief for either country. English navigators had discovered their own route to North America, and had tried to establish colonies there. English merchant-adventurers sometimes ambushed Spanish ships at sea, capturing their precious cargoes of American treasure. Despite strong protests from Spain, Queen Elizabeth I of England refused to punish these merchant-adventurers.

The help given by the English to the Dutch rebels provoked Spain to action. In 1588, Spain sent a fleet of more than 100 ships, called the Great Armada, to invade England and establish a Catholic ruler on the English throne. But a combination of stormy weather and English seamanship defeated the Great Armada and most of its ships were wrecked.

Empires in India

In some ways, the arrival of Europeans in India at the end of the 16th century marked the loss of Indian independence until the

An English merchant-adventurer

One of the greatest of the English merchant-adventurers was the soldier, sea captain and explorer, Francis Drake. Born around 1540, Drake first went to sea while still a child. In the 1560s he was raiding the coast of West Africa for slaves, much to the annoyance of the Portuguese. When he tried to sell the slaves to the Spanish in Mexico, they shot at him. Making his escape, Drake declared his own personal war on Spain.

On 13th December 1577, Drake set out to raid Spanish ships in the Pacific Ocean. Drake sailed in the *Pelican*, which was later renamed the *Golden Hind*, with several other ships under his command. Late in 1578, he finally succeeded in entering the Pacific Ocean. Only the *Golden Hind* remained, two ships had sunk in storms and others had turned back. For several months he sailed northwards along the American coast. He reached Vancouver Island in Canada, and doubled back to what is now San Francisco. Laden with captured treasure, Drake then set out across the Pacific Ocean.

The *Golden Hind*

Reaching the Spice Islands, Drake added six tonnes of illegal spices to his cargo. He then sailed back to England, arriving on 26th September 1580 to a hero's welcome, which included a knighthood from Queen Elizabeth. He was the first sea captain to complete a circumnavigation of the globe (because Magellan died halfway through his voyage). In 1588 Drake sailed with the English fleet that defeated the Spanish Armada. He died in 1596.

Babur, the first Mogul emperor of India

middle of the 20th century. However, at first the Europeans had little to do with this. In 1504, northern India was invaded from Afghanistan by the Islamic Moguls, led by Babur, a descendant of the Mongol conqueror, Ghengis Khan. In 1526, the Sultan of Delhi was defeated in battle, and a new Mogul Empire was established. Gradually the Mogul Empire extended its control southwards, until by 1636 it was nearly as large as Asoka's Empire (see page 26).

However, the Mogul Empire was not to last, and the reasons for its destruction began thousands of kilometres away, in Europe. In 1600, a group of English merchants formed the East India Company to carry out trade with India. In 1639 they established a base at Madras, followed some years later by one at Bombay. In 1696 another base was established at Calcutta in the northeast of India. Spanish and Portuguese ships were soon beaten by English naval power, but the English found other rivals in the French and the Dutch, who had made their own way to India.

Towards the end of the 17th century, the Mogul Empire finally collapsed. This left the whole of India as a prize. After years of bitter fighting, the British defeated the French, and the British Empire in India was established. The British Empire continued to expand in other parts of the world throughout the 18th and 19th centuries.

The cultivation of tea in India was a source of enormous wealth for the British Empire.

Horizons

The following people all played a part in the development of European empires overseas:
Abel Tasman (Dutch explorer); Walter Raleigh (English colonist in America); the Pilgrim Fathers (Puritan settlers in America); Jacques Cartier (French explorer who surveyed the coast of Canada and the St Lawrence River).

The Catholic empires

Through the achievements of navigators such as Vasco da Gama and Ferdinand Magellan, Spain and Portugal were able to establish empires that stretched around the world. In doing so, they were strongly supported by the Catholic Church. During the 17th century, the power of these old Catholic empires was challenged by other, mostly Protestant, European states. In the East, the empires of Spain and Portugal were replaced by British, Dutch and French trading empires. However, the Catholic empires did not lose all of their influence.

Portugal separated from Spain in 1640, becoming an independent nation once more, and keeping some overseas territories. Brazil was ruled by Portugal until the 19th century, Goa was not returned to India until 1961, and the Portuguese colonies in Africa did not receive independence until 1975.

Spain retained possession of much of Central and South America until the middle of the 19th century. In the Pacific, the Philippine Islands were transferred to the United States after the end of the Spanish-American War of 1898. The Philippines finally gained their independence at the end of World War II.

Although Magellan and Drake had sailed across the Pacific Ocean and around the world, there were still places to be discovered. Since the time of Ancient Greece, there had been legends about a great southern continent (*Terra Australis* in Latin). In the centuries to come, navigators such as James Cook would complete the exploration of the southern oceans.

A Dutch settlement in the East Indies (probably on one of the islands of Indonesia) pictured in the 17th century. The people in the street include Europeans, natives of the island and Chinese merchants.

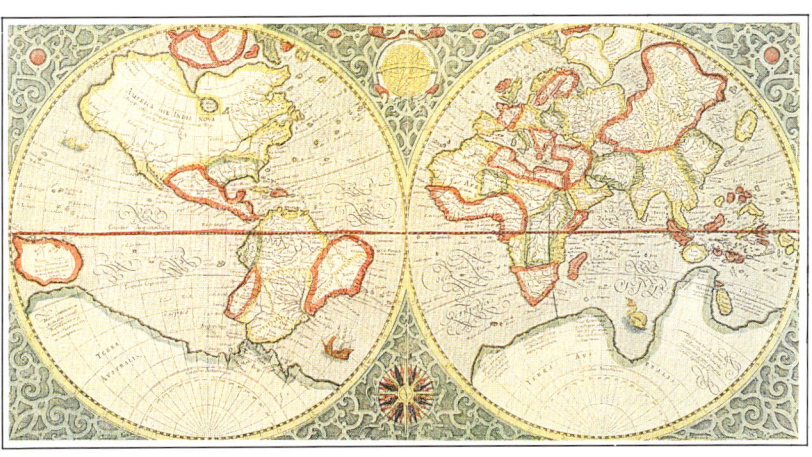

The Age of Discovery enabled Europeans to produce the first true world maps. Although the coastline is not always the correct shape, this map of 1587 is basically correct. The great unknown continent, *Terra Australis* is shown to the south.

Glossary

Arabs The people who speak Arabic, and who live on the Arabian Peninsula and in North Africa.
Buddhism An eastern religion founded in India about 2,500 years ago.
capitalism The idea of using money to make more money, either through banking or through commerce.
caravel A type of small wooden sailing ship used by many explorers during the 15th and 16th centuries.
carrack A large wooden sailing ship, the standard warship or merchant ship of the 15th and 16th centuries.
commerce Buying and selling goods on a large scale.
dhow A traditional sailing boat built by the people who live around the Indian Ocean.
factory In the Far East, this word had a special meaning a combination of office and storehouse.
Filipino A native inhabitant of the Phillipine Islands.
Hinduism The main religion of India; its followers are known as Hindus.
Jainism A minor Indian religion.
junk A traditional Chinese sailing ship.
keel The beam or girder that runs along the underside of a boat or ship, helping to keep it upright in the water.
Moguls A Central Asian people who invaded India and set up an empire in the 16th century.
Moluccas The Spice Islands situated off the east coast of India.
Moors The name given to the North African people who invaded Spain in the eighth century.
Moslem Belonging to the Islamic religion.
mutiny A rebellion by soldiers or sailors against their officers.
navigation The skill of steering a correct course between two places.
out-rigger A float attached by poles to the side of a canoe or boat.
pilot An experienced sailor responsible for guiding ships in and out of harbour.
Polynesians The people who settled on many of the Pacific islands.
rudder A steering device at the back of a ship or boat.
scurvy A disease caused by a lack of vitamin C.
Spice Islands See Moluccas
subcontinent The landmass that is now divided into India, Pakistan and Bangladesh.
sub-Saharan South of the Sahara Desert.
sultan An eastern title for a king or emperor.

Index

Africa 7-9, 12, 14, 16, 18-20, 22-25, 41, 43
Arabs 9, 16, 23, 24, 27
Asoka 26, 27
astrolabe 15

Balboa, Ferdinand 30
Benin 24
Brazil 11, 21, 28, 43
British Empire 42, 43
Buddha 26, 27

Cabral, Pedros 19, 21
Calicut 20, 21
cannon 12, 15, 21, 29
Cape of Good Hope 19, 20, 28, 33
caravel 12, 14, 15
carrack 12-15, 17
Chad, Lake 22, 24
China 4, 10, 16, 36, 38
cinnamon 4, 9, 11
cloves 4, 9, 11, 33, 37, 39
Columbus, Christopher 4, 10
Congo River 7, 8

dhow 16, 17, 23
Diaz, Bartholomew 7, 9, 18
Dutch Empire 40, 43

East India Company 42
England 6, 17, 41, 42

Filipinos 35, 36
France 6, 17, 39, 42

Gao (Africa) 22, 24
galleon 17
Gambia River 22, 24
Ganges River 26
ginger 9, 11, 32
Goa (India) 38, 43
gold 8-10, 21-25, 31, 32, 39
Guam 31
Gupta Empire 27

Hinduism 26, 27

India 4, 10, 11, 16, 21, 25-27, 38, 41-43
Indonesia 9, 43
Indus River 25
Islam 6, 7, 20, 22-24, 27, 39, 42

Jenne 22, 23

Kushan Empire 27

limes 14

mace 37
Mali 24
Mauryan Empire 26
Mediterranean Sea 6, 7, 12, 22, 38-40
Mogul Empire 42
Moluccas 9, 28, 36, 37 (see also Spice Islands)
Moors 6, 7, 10

Netherlands 6, 40, 41
Niger River 22, 24
Nok (people) 23
nutmeg 4, 9, 11, 37

Ottoman Turks 39, 40
outrigger 17, 35

Pacific Ocean 28, 30, 31, 35-37, 39, 40
padrão 14, 19, 20
Patagonia 34, 35
penguins 35
pepper 4, 9, 11
Philip II 40
Philippine Islands 28, 32, 35, 36, 39, 40, 43

Polo, Marco 4, 9, 37
Polynesians 35

rhea 35

Sahara Desert 7, 8, 22, 23
Sahel 22-24
scurvy 14, 20, 31
Senegal River 22, 24
slaves 8, 9, 16, 24, 41
Sonyhay Empire 24
Spice Islands 11, 20, 28, 32, 33, 36, 37, 41
spices 4, 6, 9-11, 20, 21, 27, 28, 36, 37, 39, 41
Sri Lanka 27, 38
Strait of Magellan 28, 29
Sultanate of Delhi 27, 42

tea 42
Timbuktu 22, 24

Venice 6, 11, 40

Zambezi River 19, 20, 25
Zanzibar 16, 22, 23
Zimbabwe 22, 25